KC/ Dec. 29/15

 W9-ANJ-815

Egypt

The Eternal Spirit of Its People

Stories of an Exhibition

by Jack Jonathan

Text by Sheelagh Hope, Inkjet Prints by Steve Barr

Melagrana Editions

Egypt, The Eternal Spirit of Its People

© JIJonathan 1952 and 2015

First Edition

No part of this publication may be reproduced,
stored in a retrieval system or transmitted, in any
form or by any means – electronic, mechanical,
photocopying, recording or otherwise – without
prior written permission from the publisher, except
for the inclusion of brief quotations in a review.

ISBN: 978-0-578-17159-3

10 9 8 7 6 5 4 3 2 1

Printed in the United States of America

Melagrana Editions

Kansas City, MO

Autumn 2015

Preface

Stories of an Exhibition

All exhibitions have a catalogue – a listing of pictures, titles, and captions. The Bibliotheca Alexandrina is producing such a document for my exhibition, *Egypt, The Eternal Spirit of Its People.*

This book is my story about the sights and experiences of growing up in Egypt more than sixty-four years ago. It documents how I became a photographer and why, in 1952, I created *Scenes of Egypt*, the first exhibition of my work in Cairo and Alexandria.

The story continues with an account of how this retrospective exhibition was created and the serendipity that lead to the exhibition at the Bibliotheca Alexandrina in Alexandria, January 2016.

Born in Egypt in 1921, I am still deeply connected to the images of the people, landscapes, and activities shown in the photographs. The captions and the stories accompanying these images are a memoir – not only my personal stories, but also my memories of growing up in Cairo in the 20's, 30's and 40's.

This is not a commentary on the Egypt of today. I have not been in my homeland since I left in 1952, so what I know of the country is what anyone can read.

To my surprise, Egyptians who have seen my photographs are delighted to discover this part of their history. They have asked me to share my stories of growing up in Egypt. They are curious about the people and places that are not often seen, or in some cases, are no longer there.

Enjoy this excursion into my past. I hope it will be meaningful to you.

Moving Still Waters: The Renaissance of the Bibliotheca Alexandrina

By Ben Proffer

The ancient Library of Alexandria was founded by Ptolemy II. The largest collection of knowledge that had ever existed, it was situated across the Bay of Alexandria from the Pharos Lighthouse, another wonder of the ancient world. By the time Julius Caesar visited the library in 48 BCE, it had amassed more than 700 thousand papyrus scrolls, and more than 128 thousand books. It burnt to the ground centuries ago.

The Bibliotheca's Reading Room

Lost, but never forgotten, the mantle of the Library of Alexandria is not carried lightly. The director who has seen the Bibliotheca Alexandrina through its first decade, Dr. Ismail Serageldin, has nothing but the highest expectations for its mission. It is to be: "The window of the world on Egypt; the window of Egypt on the world; an instrument for rising to the digital challenge; and a center for dialogue between peoples and civilizations."

It is a monumental structure with the largest reading room in the world. The reading room spans terraces on seven levels, lit by an immense ceiling of skylights. The library is a timeline of the history of knowledge. Represented here are the many ways that mankind has tried to preserve and pass on its knowledge.

Now, computers and the Internet facilitate the access to worldwide knowledge; so the architects of the Library of Alexandria designed it to be a center for the digital age. Supercomputers work somewhere in the Bibliotheca Alexandrina's four basement levels, constantly reading and recording the entirety of the Internet: Every new web page, every new pixel that comes into existence around the globe is stored using these vast machines. Whereas the ancient Library sought to be the largest

Three exterior walls of the library are inscribed with hieroglyphs and letters from all the world's languages, alluding to the library's ancient heritage.

collection of knowledge, the new Bibliotheca seeks to be the storehouse of all knowledge.

However, the scope of its intellectual and literary collection is only part of the Library's mission; it was also designed to be a center for dialogue. "It was created to help move still waters, and to try to improve the performance of things through getting the people, the parties, maybe, opposing parties, together, not specifically political," explained Gamal Hosni, its Director of Art Exhibitions and Collections. Honeycombed around the reading room are galleries that house permanent and visiting exhibitions, where the Bibliotheca displays the finest art from around the world and ages past.

In a world where communication and intellectual exchange have no friction, and no physical center, the Bibliotheca Alexandrina acts as a guiding star to everyone who longs to understand and be understood. At a time when the world is facing the darkest form of radical extremism, we look to the strongholds of enlightenment such as the Bibliotheca Alexandrina to nurture and safeguard intellectual freedom.

Stationed as a lighthouse before a world in a tempest, the Bibliotheca Alexandrina offers to the courageous mind and steady heart the security of our shared wisdom, past and future.

Surrounded by water, the library's tilted disk shape suggests the sun on the Mediterranean horizon.

Acknowledgments

When one dreams alone, it may only be a dream.
      When we dream together, it is the beginning of reality.

Jack Jonathan

I owe my success to the people who have participated in my projects over the years. How fortunate I am, at this time in my life, to be surrounded by a truly marvelous team.

The three principals who helped me produce this book have worked with me for ten years or more. Frank Addington designed all but one of the *Yes, You Can* books. Steve Barr created the inkjet prints for my 2004 exhibition, *Light is the Eye of The Mind*, for the benefit of the Stowers Institute for Medical Research. More recently, he printed the photographs for the *Healing Images* installation at Children's Mercy Hospital, and the current exhibition, *Egypt, The Eternal Spirit of Its People*. Since 2004, Sheelagh Hope has collaborated with me to write four of the *Yes, You Can* books, Jim Stowers' autobiography, and several children's stories. She wrote the text for *Egypt, The Eternal Spirit of Its People: Stories of an Exhibition*.

For the last seven years Marc Plowman has kept us on the straight and narrow with our computers. Glenda Spellerberg, who provided us with care and support in every aspect of our business, is now our trusted bookkeeper. Recently she was joined by Lindsey Whitely who elegantly organizes the office and has become "my eyes." There is a great deal to do and fortunately Lindsey is a quick learner.

We owe the opportunity to mount this exhibition to Proffer Productions, and in particular, Ben Proffer, who is the agent in charge of my photographic exhibitions. This spring he carried the 90 prints to Alexandria and will help to make things smooth when we attend the exhibition there in January of 2016.

This exhibition would not be possible without the enthusiastic appreciation for my work expressed by Hanan El Badry and Dr. Ismael Serageldin, founder and director of the Bibliotheca Alexandrina. *Egypt, The Eternal Spirit of Its People* became a reality when a team was assigned to organize an exhibition at the Bibliotheca in Alexandria. We are grateful to this team of helpful, welcoming people: Hoda El Mikaty, Gamal Hosni, Marc Henine, Iman Hosny, Mohamed Khamis, Mohamed Hesham Elzohery, Khaled Elkardy and Mahoud Hagras. They have made my dream a reality.

Sheelagh and I are grateful to our family members whom we always prevail upon to read our manuscripts. My sons, Steve and David Jonathan, are tough critics, but in the end that works to our advantage. Sheelagh's daughters, Catriona Briger and Hillary Urich, and her granddaughter, Francesca Manheim, are kinder but no less critical in their reviews.

Many friends have risen to the occasion and consented to read our manuscript. Thank you, Alexis Preston, Sam Goller, Bruce Bradley, Dan Foster, Jim Ramirez, Dr. Hesham Soliman, Webb Schott, Mary Lynn Soli Mikhail, John Small, and Aundrea Whitely, for taking time out of your own busy lives to enrich ours.

Finally, I want to lovingly acknowledge the two women who have been by my side most of my life. My dear little sister, Miriam, began working for me in Cairo when she was only 18. Now in her eighties, I still rely on her elegant language skills to help polish our work.

My beloved wife of sixty-four years, Rena, was there as I struggled to showcase my work as a photographer. It was she who, through her contacts with the Fulbright Foundation in Cairo, found the space for the 1952 *Scenes of Egypt* exhibition. She reads all that I write, and her gentle criticism provides much support.

CONTENTS

Preface..3

Moving Still Waters:
The Renaissance of Bibliotheca Alexandrina **by Ben Proffer** 4

Acknowledgments..6

PART I **Thriving in a Time of Chaos, 1939 - 1952**.......11

The Story Begins... 12

Foreword: **Immigrants to Egypt, 1919** by Sheelagh Hope...............12

Apprenticeship 15

Mastering the Arts of Printing and Photography..........................19

My Graduate Thesis: Creating an Exhibition, Scenes of Egypt..........27

Afterword: **1952: A New Life Begins in the United States** by Sheelagh Hope 36

The Story Continues... 48

A Retrospective Exhibition, 2016 48

PART II **Egypt, The Eternal Spirit of Its People:**
Stories of an Exhibition 45

Introduction: **Seeing Into The Heart of Things** 50

Egypt's Timeless Environment 53

Land of the Pharaohs...54

Strolling Through Old Cairo 62

The Eternal Spirit of the People 72

Faces of Old Cairo 74

Egypt – The Gift of the Nile 91

The Land and Its People 113

A Glimpse of Bedouin Life 142

Biographies of My Team 160

Creating the Book Specifications 162

"If you cannot achieve your ideal,
Idealize your real."

Jack Jonathan

PART I

Thriving in a Time of Chaos

The Story Begins…

Foreword: **Immigrants to Egypt, 1919** By Sheelagh Hope

Jack Jonathan's temperament was forged in the furnace of the political chaos that followed World War I. The failure of the monarchies plunged Europe into uncertainty, as leaders of each nation wrestled with creating a political system that would fulfill their ambitions. The political turmoil spilled over into Egypt, the cosmopolitan crossroads of western and eastern cultures and home, not only to Egyptians, but also to French, Italian, Greek, English, and other minorities.

Jack was born in 1921 to Sephardic Jewish parents who moved to Egypt from Palestine in 1919. As in some other homes in the city, the conversation during the Jonathan's evening meal was in a veritable Babel of languages. The parents spoke to the children in French and conversed with each other in Spanish or Hebrew. The boys, who attended an Italian elementary school, argued with each other in Italian. After his sisters began their schooling at the English Mission College, they chatted to each other in English.

Jack was an active boy whose defining challenge was an accident that shattered his left leg when he was thirteen. His father used Jack's enforced six-month confinement as an opportunity to challenge the mind of his restless son by bringing home every book on history and adventure he could find.

When he was choosing his educational focus at boarding school in Alexandria, Jack wanted to focus on accounting so he could help his father in his business. However, his father wisely insisted that Jack take courses that would earn him a baccalaureate. He advised his second born son that, *"A classical education will last you a lifetime and will give you the discipline to learn anything you need to learn."* Jack's curious mind delighted in this course of studies. He was not a passive learner, he loved spending time in the library reading and doing research. One day, it took his fancy to write an adventure story about Australia. During the lunch meal, the boys took turns reading aloud as the others ate their soup. When it was his turn, Jack courageously read his own work, passing it off as a published book. So professional and engaging was the story that everyone but his teacher was fooled. The next morning, Jack found a note on his desk: "Shorter sentences."

During his high school years, Jack was enrolled at the Royal Italian Lyceum in Cairo where he expected to be excused from the obligatory sports program because of his noticeable limp. However, the coach insisted that he participate. It soon became clear that even with a limp, Jack was a natural athlete.

In 1938, Jack became a valued member and captain of the school's 4 x 100 meter relay team. Their coach, who had attended the 1936 Olympics in Berlin, inspired the young men with a film of the gold medal win of the American 4 x 100 relay team led by Jesse Owens. In secret, they practiced the U.S. team's unique technique of passing the baton at top speed. The team was fired up, hoping this technique would give them an edge in the Royal Egyptian National Championship.

Jack

Winners of the 1938 Egyptian National Championship
4 x 100 meter relay race.

Sure enough, their secret skill enabled them to beat out faster runners from the Royal Guard and the University to win the championship. Their reward was a trip to Rome, Italy, to participate in an all-Italian track meet arranged to try out the new track built for the ill-fated 1940 Olympics.

Germany declared war in September of 1939, and Cairo, "host" to countries on both sides of the conflict, was thrown into chaos. A few weeks after the war began, Jack's world, too, was turned upside down when his father died unexpectedly, leaving the family of seven children with no means of support. Destined for the university after his final year at the Royal Italian Lyceum, Jack left school to join his older brother in earning the family livelihood.

Many young people facing two such great challenges would feel overwhelmed. Jack, however, was made of sterner stuff. He rose to the challenge of providing for his family and took on the best opportunity offered to him. As you read his story, you will see this theme repeated over and over: Jack reframes his obstacles, looks for opportunities, chooses the best, and then works diligently to succeed. One of his favorite adages is, ***"If you cannot achieve your ideal, idealize your real."***

Apprenticeship

When I was 18 and in my last year at the Royal Italian Lyceum in Cairo, my Dad died. His death left our family without an income, so it was up to my older brother and me to work to support the family. Two of my dad's friends offered to help me find a job. One said, "I can get you a job as an accountant with the Shell Oil Company in Cairo." The other said, "If you want to learn the printing business, you can get started any time."

I was totally unprepared to earn a living in a specific trade because, on the advice of my Dad, I had chosen the classics curriculum over accounting courses. Later in life, Dad's wisdom proved to be right: my philosophy, logic, and language studies were critical to my success. Now, however, I just needed to earn a living any way I could. I chose the road less traveled, the printing industry, and that made all the difference in my life.

At first I was an apprentice with the British company, John Dickinson, the largest Middle East importer of paper, printing equipment, and supplies. When he hired me, the manager laid out the facts, "Even though you have a good education, you are not worth very much." Offering me a salary that was less than we paid our servant, he continued, "Here are a bunch of catalogues in English, French and German. Learn what's in these catalogues and ask questions about the equipment we have on display. I'll test you every 90 days and give you a raise if you can sell me a piece of our equipment." This was all the incentive I needed. Within a year I had earned three raises, each one almost double my starting salary.

I learned how to sell printing equipment, supplies, paper, ink, and binding equipment. I found my way around all the printers in Cairo and Alexandria and within a year I knew what was going on in the printing industry.

During the time I worked in the showroom learning the products, I was asked to take care of the stationery needs of the department. My first responsibility was to reorder an internal memo for the *machinery department.* When the simple form of three lines was shown to me for approval, I skimmed over it and signed off on the run. The next day, the manager showed me the forms. There, glaring at me, was *Machinery Pepartment.* I was humiliated and wanted to redo the run, but my manager saw a teaching moment. "No, we will use them. There are 2,000 of these and it will take us about two years to use them all up; this will be a reminder for everyone of the importance of being careful when approving something."

That incident has stayed with me all my life. Many times I have used this embarrassing incident to inspire the people who work with me to pay attention to the small details that make a job look professional. I know now that in this apprenticeship I was a *Printer's Devil.* There are many stories about where this term comes from. The one I remember is:

In the early days of moveable type, circa 1500, there was a pious monk who had written a book called "Anatomy of the Mass." So numerous were the blunders when the book was printed that the errata was almost as long as the original text. The worthy monk, understandably chagrined, prefaced the errata with an apology that laid the blame for the mistakes on Satan. That the Devil had his tail deep in the brew of printing was a common belief in the early days of the craft. And so it was that struggling apprentices became known as Printer's Devils.

The year 1940 was a turning point for me. On June 2, my 19th birthday, I received my baccalaureate from the Royal Italian Lyceum. Two days later, after Italy joined Germany in the war against the Allies, an Italian distributor for the Intertype Corporation in Alexandria committed an act of sabotage. He tore the catalogues, took the tags off the spare parts, and threw the lot, along with 60,000 matrices, into a big hole. Then he escaped to join the Italian forces.

After the Turks were defeated in World War I, Egypt became a sovereign country under the protection of England. So when the Italians allied with Germany in WWII, England took temporary possession of the Italian properties in Egypt; and John Dickinson, an English company, became the new managing entity of the properties owned by the Italian Intertype Corporation. The English manager called me to his office. Speaking in broken English interspersed with Italian and a little French he tired to help me understand the situation and gave me an opportunity. "Go to Alexandria and pick up the mess. When you put it back in order, you'll be the exclusive salesman for Intertype!"

During the war there were very few imports, so our company had to make do by trading around with what was available. During my first year with John Dickinson, I had become familiar with the needs and wants of the printers who remained in business. Since the Intertype machine was essential equipment for all the newspapers and publishers, my manager's offer was an incredible opportunity for me!

I went to Alexandria, took the Intertype mess out of the dump, packed it in boxes, put it on a truck, and drove it to Cairo. There, in the poorly lit basement of John Dickinson, I laboriously sorted out the 60,000 matrices by font size, character and style.

What is a Matrix?

A matrix is the heart of the Intertype composing machine. It is the typeface mold for the newspapers that is used to produce a slug of lead that represents one line of type – hence, linotype. Imagine a typewriter connected to a storage tank that holds 90 channels, each of which is loaded with 10 – 15 matrices. All the matrices looked alike, yet they were coded differently. Intertype, for example, offered a selection of typefaces in 6, 8, 10, or 12 point sizes with different font styles. I had to identify and sort the matrices by character, type style and font size. Then, each one had to be put into the proper type cases.

Using glassine adhesive strips, I patched together the ripped catalogues so I could identify the spare parts and re-label them. It took me three months to get everything back in order. Let me tell you, if I were to say to any of my children, "This is how you get started in life," they would surely ask me, "Is it worth it?"

I would tell them, "You do whatever you need to do to survive."

By the time I was finished, I knew the parts of the Intertype machine very well, but I didn't know how to operate it. Max Koch, a German refugee who was the superintendent of the commercial printer and publisher of La Bourse Egyptiènne invited me to come to the night shift to practice operating a Linotype machine that was similar to the Intertype machine in quality and function.

After I had learned to operate the Intertype machine and demonstrate its capabilities to customers, John Dickinson made me the exclusive Intertype salesman for Egypt. I was only 20 years old. Hoping to present a more mature image, I grew a moustache.

Mastering the Arts of Printing and Photography

The United States Office of War Information

The next big turning point in my career came in 1942. The United States Office of Strategic Services established a beachhead in Cairo with a focus on intelligence work. John Dickinson lent me to the U.S. as an advisor on issues relating to printing and production.

In 1943, needing to implement psychological warfare strategies, the United States Office of War Information (US-OWI) was established and I was offered a permanent job. The OWI in Cairo was like a huge advertising/public relations agency staffed with sixty professionals who were too old to carry a gun. Instead, they focused their unique talents on the war effort. They were writers, editors, photographers and illustrators, who proved every day that the pen is mightier than the sword.

My department was in the basement of the Embassy. This space was set up as a small printing shop fitted with offset lithography presses and a small bindery. I started working as the gofer for an American in charge of printing and production. I learned a lot from him. Unfortunately, he loved the high life, so I would have to cover for him when he arrived very late in the morning. Sometimes, if I needed his approval on something, I would go over to his hotel with papers for him to sign. One day he greeted me with a despicable slur. That was it for me. I decided to resign.

I went to the Chief of the OWI, Oscar Dystel, who later became the president of Bantam Publishing. Oscar said to me, "Stay, Jack. We'll fix it." The manager was sent back to the States within 48 hours and I began working more than 12 hours a day as the interim manager of printing and production. Because of its highly confidential nature, the position of manager was a prerogative reserved for U.S. citizens. However, within a year, I became the first non-American manager.

Psychological warfare work was fascinating and intense. Here is an example of our work in action.

Illustrator Johnny Pike, a famous watercolorist, would create a poster to encourage resistance in areas occupied by Germany. I would roll up his watercolor and fly to Alexandria to a printer/lithographer whom I knew from my days with John Dickinson. Walter Scharff, a refugee from Germany, would call in his key lithographers who would carefully examine the artwork for the poster. They might conclude, "We need at least 12 colors to do this. When do you need them?" I might say, "48 hours." The team would then work 48 hours without a break! When the posters were ready, they would be rolled up, put into canisters and flown out of Cairo to be dropped behind enemy lines. To help the local patriots fight the Nazis, we developed a case that held ink, paper and an 8" x 10" hand-platen printing press with moveable type in Italian, Cyrillic and Greek. These were also parachuted behind enemy lines so that the underground could create their own propaganda locally.

The United States Information Service

In 1945, after Victory in Europe Day, there was quite a change. Did we close shop? No, because a different kind of war began - the Cold War, a war of words. It was a new era; the British influence in Egypt and the Middle East was slowly eroding. The Americans stepped into the vacuum to protect the region from the influence of communism. The United States Information Service (USIS, now called the USIA, United States Information Agency) was founded to promote democracy in the Middle East.

By then I was in charge of the Printing and Publications Department located in the basement of the Embassy compound in Cairo. Many of the people who had come to help with the war effort left and

Publications 1946 — 1952

USIS Books and Pamphlets

Simple Parliamentary Procedure

Self-Government USA

4-H Club

Constitution of the U.S.A.

Outline of History

The Art of the Libraries in Service of the Youth

The Free World Speaks Up, Illustrated cartoon style

Toys at Home and Children's Preschool Toys

How the U.S.A. was Established

Translations of American Literature into Arabic

My Antonia by Willa Cather

America by Stephen Vincent Benet

Animal Farm by George Orwell

Huckleberry Finn by Mark Twain

The Autobiography of George Washington Carver

Amelia Earhart: The Kansas Girl by Jane Moore Howe

Up Above and Down Below by Irma Webber

were replaced by talented professionals: writers, librarians and public relations experts. A model library was established at the Embassy to promote the values of the United States. The Book Translation Program produced library science books, as well as pamphlets, booklets and American literature in Arabic that were distributed to other key cities in the Middle East. For me, it was like going to college.

The translating process was a complicated business. For official documents such as the Constitution, the Egyptian team would translate the text from English to Arabic. Then, because we wanted to be sure the translations were accurate, another team would re-translate the "official" document back into English to make sure that the meanings were not lost.

Beautiful books designed with a variety of typefaces have always delighted me, so I was frustrated by the limited Arabic fonts available to us. They were not as decorative as comparable choices in English. I solved this problem by using standard Arabic fonts for the body of the work and then hiring a scribe to write titles and headings in Arabic. The results were aesthetically pleasing.

The reputation of our work was unique, especially when we published popular books. Partly due to the marvelous illustrations of a local cartoonist, one of the most successful was *Animal Farm* by the British author George Orwell. With our limited facilities, we produced sample editions that were distributed to all the other U.S. embassies in the Arab world. Once their orders were placed, we launched a public edition in partnership with a local publisher.

The Free World Speaks Up

Amelia Earhart: The Kansas Girl by Jane Moore Howe

Animal Farm by George Orwell

The Art of the Libraries in Service of the Youth

My Passion for Photography

Being Chief of Printing and Publications for the USIS and the American Embassy in Cairo was challenging. I thrived on the opportunity to create a high quality service. To reach my goal of excellence, I needed to understand all aspects of the job. Yet, one area was a mystery to me – photography.

At that time a photographer did not just take pictures; he controlled the entire photographic process from shooting, to developing, to printing. In our department, this work was done by a guild of three skillful Armenians who jealously protected the secrets of the craft that was their livelihood. I sometimes challenged the photographer, "Is this the best you can do?" Always he would assure me that nothing more could be done.

I was polite because I did not understand the process. It quickly became clear that to make improvements, I would need to get a camera and learn how to shoot and print negatives. Our lab technician, Artine Der Balian, had a Vöigtlander camera – an early model that was followed later by the dual-lens Rolleiflex. One evening, as I was approving some photographs for release to the press attaché, I asked Artine if he was interested in selling his Vöigtlander. I offered him twice the market value provided that he sell me his camera and also teach me how to process and print negatives.

On the condition that we do it after hours, Artine began demonstrating the fine points of creating good finished prints. He was an excellent teacher and I was an avid student. Within two months I was ready to experiment on my own.

Buying the Vöigtlander from Artine gave me an entry into the world of photography. However, it was the purchase of my dream camera, a Rolleiflex, which freed my imagination because the faster shutter speed allowed me to take candid shots even with limited light. The camera, an extension of my eyes, became my constant companion. I practiced often and eagerly awaited the evening hours to see what would unfold in the dark room.

My understanding of the art of photography took a leap forward around 1947 when the *Life Magazine* photographer, David Douglas Duncan, a native of Kansas City, stopped by the embassy in Cairo on his way home from the war in Korea. Duncan's approach was unique. Using the familiar German Leica camera fitted with the fastest lens of that era, a Japanese Nikon 1.2 lens, he shot his images in difficult conditions without a flash. To ensure that the film would reveal the underexposed images, he boosted the film speed from 100 ASA to 400 ASA. This innovative approach to capturing images required an equally innovative approach to developing the film. David borrowed my lab so he could have creative control of the development of the negatives, thus assuring the quality of his effort.

David's visits meant a great deal to me because we exchanged ideas about what it takes to create a good image. He shot photos on the move without elaborate preparations or posing of his subjects. He had an amazing ability to frame his shots and anticipate the exact moment to snap the shutter, capturing an image that vibrated with an immediacy that was difficult to achieve.

In 1947, the tensions in the Middle East were on the rise. A person who took photographs outdoors would arouse suspicion. However, in my official capacity as Chief of Publications at the Embassy, I had some wonderful photographic opportunities. Jefferson Caffery, the American Ambassador, loved to go on excursions to visit the area west of Cairo known for its antiquities – his favorites being the pyramids and the Sphinx. His personal secretary, Robert Simpson, often invited me to go along on these outings. While the Ambassador was climbing the pyramids, I roamed among the latest archeological digs. It was here that I captured some of my most memorable images.

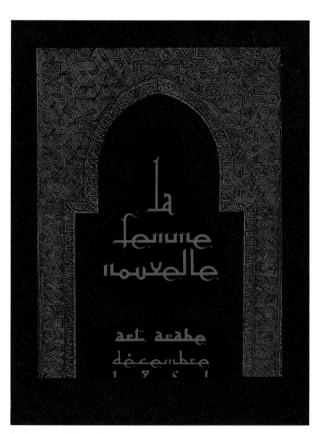

La Femme Nouvelle

Later, in 1950, Doria Shafik, the feminist editor of a French cultural and literary magazine, *La Femme Nouvelle*, asked me to illustrate a feature story about the mosques in Cairo. The historian, Gaston Wiet, whom I accompanied around Old Cairo, was a fount of knowledge about the beautiful old structures. He would point to a mosque and enlighten me about the building's history while I looked around for the most favorable angle to photograph. Our article appeared in the magazine's December 1951 edition, *Art Arabe*.

The opportunity to photograph the monuments and buildings of this ancient city was like a dream come true for me. Buildings have moods. The texture of the stone, etched by the sun and rain and wind, speaks of centuries of history. I was fascinated by the way the light and shadow fell on the ancient monuments – the way they totally changed as the sun crossed the sky, lighting up what had been dark, revealing what had been hidden.

Later, alone in my lab, I would play with the images, trying a variety of techniques to draw out aspects that I had overlooked when I first captured the scene. Can I get more details of a dim corner? Ah, there, emerging from the developing bath I could see the steps that were once hidden in the shadows. I was fascinated by the details that revealed themselves in the silence of my dark room.

My work with Artine and my long sessions in the lab with David Douglas Duncan heightened my awareness that capturing memorable images was only part of the work of a photographer. Like David, I found that to create a superb photograph, I needed to have control over the whole process.

My Graduate Thesis: Creating a Photographic Exhibition

A Changing Political Climate for Egypt

In 1950, I was invited to visit the States to participate in an orientation established by the State Department for the benefit of "alien" employees of the USIS. Focused on learning about advances in the printing, publishing, and photographic industries, I planned to visit places in the U.S. that were on the cutting edge of these industries. Because the State Department wanted me to become familiar with a small American college, my tour began in Massachusetts at Springfield College, famous for sports and James Naismith who invented basketball. During my first evening in Springfield, I was giving a speech at the college about my life in Egypt when I spotted a lovely woman in the front row. Rena Della Libera captured my heart not only with her beauty, but also with her passion for knowledge, and her love of dancing. After sixty-four years of marriage, I am still amazed that, after only a brief courtship, she agreed to marry me. Three months after we met, she accompanied me back to Cairo, where we explored the Egypt of my childhood. Unfortunately, this carefree time was short lived.

After World War II, the Egyptians were still living in a world dominated by European interests. The corrupt politicians, the King's self-serving staff, and a monarch who was famous for his skills as a poker player, were a great disappointment to the people. The Egyptian army, inspired by Lt. Col. Gamal Nasser, slowly began to plan the long awaited dream of an Egypt free of foreign influences. A day after a clash between British troops and police left fifty Egyptian policemen dead in Ismailia, a riot erupted in Cairo.

An early morning ride on our anniversary, January 1952.

Rena and I were celebrating our first wedding anniversary at the world famous Shepheard's Hotel located near the opera house on the western side of the city. We dined and danced before slowly walking home. From our 7th floor apartment we heard the piercing screams of sirens. We rushed to the window and saw the horizon light up – the western half of Cairo was ablaze. The army, called in to restore order, declared martial law and set up a 6 p.m. curfew. The 1952 revolution had begun. It was a dangerous, traumatic time.

My family, who lived in Heliopolis 20 miles east of Cairo, was not immediately affected by the chaos. However, Rena and I, aware of the difficulties of raising a family in an unstable political environment, decided to accelerate our return to the United States. How fortunate that we had somewhere to go.

The decision having been made, an important question arose, "How would I earn a living?" By 1952, 13 years after I began as a Printer's Devil, I would be leaving the USIS fully qualified to take up a career in graphic arts and publishing. But there was another appealing option – perhaps I could use this move as an opportunity to change my career and realize my dream of earning a living as a photographer like David Douglas Duncan.

In order to make this option a viable one, I would need some evidence that I was a photographer of worth. I decided to showcase my talent by creating a photographic exhibition of what I knew best, the people and places of Cairo.

Creating the *Scenes of Egypt* Exhibition

In reviewing the collection of my photographs, I discovered there were plenty of the traditional iconic images popular with tourists: monuments, antiquities, and mosques. Missing were photographs of the daily life of the people in the city, the farmers in the rural areas along the Nile, and the Bedouins. I decided that my exhibition should feature intimate scenes of the ordinary people of Egypt that I grew up with for 30 years. I had work to do!

For the next three months, I put in nearly 20 hours a day to fit in my busy schedule at the Embassy and my own work of shooting, developing, and selecting the right images. I took side trips to villages around Cairo and to the desert. At this time of political strife, it was not always safe to wander around taking photographs, so an escort from the tourist bureau sometimes accompanied me.

In my early years, when we lived on a dairy farm, I befriended the fellaheen (peasants) and their families who lived at the edge of the desert by the irrigation canal. Now, fifteen years later, I sought to reconnect with some of the moments I had experienced in the past. This was not easy since most people in Egypt, cautious of my camera, presented a very solemn face. Yet, because I was sincerely interested in them, I was often rewarded with a special smile.

The theme of my photographic essay was "The Vigor and Beauty of Egyptian Life." After accumulating 300 wonderful images, I selected the best ones, focusing on people simply going about their lives.

My intention was to create the prints as large as possible so that people could really engage with the subjects. This was particularly important for portraits. My enlarger could only produce prints up to 11" x 14." To create larger images, innovation would be required. I experimented by turning the enlarger around and projecting the images onto the floor. Because of the quality of the enlarger's lens, I was able to extend the size to 17" x 22" while still maintaining sharpness.

Once 61 photographs were printed, I had to decide how to display them. The cost of matting and framing were beyond my limited budget, so I used the bindery facilities to mount the pictures. The bookbinder affixed the prints to binding boards with animal glue. The next morning I was faced with a small tragedy – the first mounted prints, which looked perfect the night before, had curled. My heart sank. The bookbinder kept his cool. Smiling calmly, he said, "Mr. Jonathan, don't worry, I will fix this." He proceeded to select paper of the same thickness as the print and glued it to the reverse side of the board. That simple solution corrected the curling and we proceeded to mount the remaining photographs.

My sister, Miriam, was a critical member of my USIS staff. For previous Embassy events she had developed a method for creating lovely invitations that looked as if they were engraved. To do this she had to improvise. First, she selected a sheet of beautiful English script font available for art purposes. Then, she laboriously created the whole invitation by carefully cutting each letter and mounting it on a large board. A lithographic plate was created reducing the image by a third, thus masking any minor imperfections. After it was printed, the finished product looked like an engraved invitation.

The United States Educational Foundation for Egypt
requests the pleasure of your company
at a Photographic Exhibit
Scenes of Egypt
by Isaac Jonathan
Tuesday, the 25th of March
at five o'clock

1, Sh. el Shams, Garden City   *Tel. 54438*

Back   Front

The catalogue was a challenge. In order to accommodate both people who spoke Arabic and those who spoke English, it would need to read from left to right and from right to left. In searching for the right cover, my photograph of the Al-Rifa'i Mosque jumped out at us. Its diagonal design would work perfectly with English on the front, opening right, and Arabic on the back, opening from the left.

For the English side of the cover, I used the positive print that shows the wall of the mosque in shadow. On the Arabic side of the cover, the negative image is reversed so that the wall of the mosque appears white.

Scenes of Egypt was shown twice: first, in Cairo on March 25th, 1952, at the United States Educational Foundation for Egypt; then, in Alexandria opening a month later at the Cecil Hotel, under the patronage of the American Cultural Center.

Miriam and I hung the pictures, then we waited. Would anyone come? Of course our family and friends came. However, I was surprised and gratified at the interest of the Egyptian public and the press. I was also amazed when Hafez Afifi Pasha, Head of the Egyptian Royal Cabinet, arrived. He walked around the exhibition with me asking a lot of questions. He was more than interested in my work – he ordered nine 11" x 14" prints. Because it was not public knowledge, I was unaware that the King would abdicate in July. In retrospect, it seems that Afifi Pasha carefully selected images that would remind the exiled King of his beloved Egypt.

Another distinguished visitor represented the Department of Commerce and Industry. He selected four prints for the Egyptian Pavilion at the International Conference in Barcelona, Spain.

The exhibition received positive reviews in the Arabic press as well as in English, French, and Greek journals. The Arabic press appreciated that I had captured the beauty of the country. Here is an excerpt from *Al Zamane*, an Arabic daily newspaper: *The artist expresses his appreciation for Egypt, her beauty and nature... Some of (the pictures) portray Islamic history of Egypt, others represent Egyptian country life in a very dramatic manner.*

His Excellency, Hafez Afifi Pasha, Head of the Egyptian Royal Cabinet, attends the opening of a photographic exhibit "Scenes of Egypt" by Isaac Jonathan. The exhibit was held in Cairo under the auspices of the U.S. Educational Foundation for Egypt.

Hafez Afifi Pasha selected 9 designs, totaling 34 copies in 2 different sizes. Unbeknownst to me at the time, the King was going to abdicate the throne in July, 1952.

Letter from Under Secretary of Department of Commerce, May, 1952, requesting four prints for the International Conference in Barcelona, Spain.

The weekly magazine *Al Mussawar* (The Photographer) acknowledged that I had been raised in Egypt and "felt a great sympathy for the country and her peoples." I was delighted that the critic understood my fascination with light when he said that I had "translated my feelings for my country into light and shadows."

The critic of the French paper, *La Bourse Egyptiènne*, judged the exhibition from an artistic point of view and from my choice of images – escaping "banality" and achieving "new angles" of familiar scenes. However, what I really appreciated was his understanding of the technical difficulties of shooting outdoors and my ability to overcome them. "The technique is impeccable, and that is a compliment… since most of the images were taken in bright sunlight."

A comment that touched me as deeply then as it does today was a handwritten note from Professor Abdel Rahman Fawzi who thanked me for the exhibition and wrote: "Really you have proved that the Jews and the Arabs are cousins, and I assure you that 100 wise Jews as yourself can make peace between the two Semitic cousins."

These, and other positive reviews of my work, strengthened my resolve to realize my dream of becoming a professional photographer.

المصور

Al Mussawar,
April 18, 1952

LA BOURSE EGYPTIENNE

"SCENES D'EGYPTE"
Exposition de photographies
d'Isaac Jonathan

"Isaac Jonathan, who
exhibited 60 artistic
pictures taken from
our life, did not do
more than reveal
beautiful shots which
otherwise would have
been hidden from
our eyes."

"The technique is impeccable,
and that is a compliment...
since most of the images
were taken in bright sunlight."

Afterword: **Starting Over In the United States, 1952** By Sheelagh Hope

After his successful exhibitions of *Scenes of Egypt* in Cairo and Alexandria, Jack and his wife, Rena, left Egypt for a well-deserved vacation in Europe. They arrived in Naples, where their household luggage was sent on to Le Havre. To Rena's consternation, Jack refused to relinquish two large specially designed cases in which the *Scenes of Egypt* photographs were carefully and securely nestled.

"These are my hope for the future," Jack insisted to Rena. And so, through their six-week tour of Europe, the cases were carefully carried and stored and fussed over.

The trip began with a memorable week in Florence during Maggio Musicale, a month-long celebration of the Arts. The next stop was a homecoming for Rena, a visit to Stradala and Portalbera, two small adjoining towns near the Po River where she had lived for five years as a little girl. What a delight it was for Jack to get to know Rena's Italian family. Then it was on to visit Jack's cousin in Paris. A highlight for the young couple was a very special time in Normandy where they stayed in a village near Mount St. Michel.

At the end of June they arrived at the dock in Le Havre, boarded the liner, and sailed off into their new adventure together. They relished their time at sea, each filled with a

Bridging 64 years —
from their original cases, *Scenes of Egypt* becomes
Egypt, the Eternal Spirit of Its People.

special glow of hope. They had much to talk about and plan for – the start of a new life together in a new homeland, and perhaps, a new career for Jack.

Here is Jack's account of arriving in the United States, this time as an immigrant.

The last six months of my life in Egypt were very stressful. I was leaving behind an exciting life for the unknown. As we stood on the deck watching the Statue of Liberty slowly emerging out of the morning mist, I was suddenly overwhelmed by the enormity of my decision. I exploded with feeling. Tears streamed down my face as all the pent-up emotion came out of me. I felt the sadness of leaving my family, but also relieved, grateful that we were finally here, that our life as a new family was truly about to begin.

Emotions continued to swirl through me as we walked off the ship onto Ellis Island. There was a display in one of the halls, a mound of old suitcases – a silent memorial to all the immigrants before me. Who were they? Had they succeeded? Now it was my turn to find my way and create a successful life for my family.

At the beginning of August, Jack and Rena settled in her hometown of Springfield, Massachusetts. For two weeks Jack searched for work as a photographer. Turning up empty handed, he set out for New York to pursue several leads. He was a salesman showcasing his portfolio of photographs nestled in their sample cases. It was August, hot and humid, and he was sweating in his best tweed jacket as he lugged the heavy cases from one interview to another. There were many enticing possibilities but no secure offer. Finally, with the responsibility of a first child on the way, Jack chose to avoid the uncertainty of forging a new career. Instead, he accepted an interview with a company in Cleveland, Ohio, World Publishing, known for its high quality of printing and binding of Bibles and trade books.

The interview with the president Benjamin Zevin went well enough; Jack had all the skills the company needed. Then, Mr. Zevin asked Jack about his exhibition in Cairo, and things took a different direction. Benjamin Zevin was an amateur photographer! They veered off into a discussion of cameras, and darkrooms. To Jack's surprise, along with a job, Mr. Zevin offered him his darkroom equipment. Photography, Jack's passion, was to remain in his life as an avocation. While he was in Cleveland, he taught a course in photography at the local YMCA and was able to have a small exhibition.

Jack stayed at World Publishing until he had finished with his project, introducing the first *Webster's New World Dictionary of the American Language*; a unique publication because it was printed on Bible paper, making the extensive dictionary easy to handle. However, since it was a small family company, Jack was aware that there was no room for his imagination to grow. So, in 1954, through an introduction by his friend, the renowned world traveller and photographer Jack Grover, Jack accepted a position at Hallmark Cards in Kansas City, Missouri. There he had the opportunity to integrate 15 years of experience in the graphic arts.

Under the benevolent mentorship of J.C. Hall, the founder, Jack was inspired to go beyond traditional greeting cards to create new concepts and innovations in social expression products. Within a few years, enthusiastically supported by farsighted managers and Donald Hall, Sr., Jack developed new product lines such as books, albums, calendars, and posters. He also innovated trend setting greeting card promotions including patented display units. He introduced photographs into the card line and was able to create photographic images of his own for a line of cards, *Personal Expression*.

Jack was always driven by Joyce Hall's admonition that they must constantly "create and recreate a customer." In 1970, Hallmark, challenged by an aggressive competitor, provided an outlet for Jack's entrepreneurial spirit by inviting him to set up an intrapreneurial team, "Group 71." This group, an innovative fast track within the organized framework of the big corporation, enabled Hallmark to remain on the cutting edge of the social expression business.

"Group 71" was Hallmark's first multidisciplinary creative team, combining marketing, design, editorial, and multimedia production. One of their innovations was called *The Little Gallery*. Inspired by the leader they dubbed Hurricane Jack, the team stretched the limits of the creative process in producing a collection of exquisite miniatures and collectibles in bronze, silver, pewter, wood, crystal, porcelain, fabrics, and of course, paper. Inside the Hallmark Gold Crown Stores a unique section displayed these lovely gifts. Hoping to be the first to own the latest collectible, customers would make a beeline for the *Little Gallery* whenever they visited the store.

Hallmark was a wonderland for a person with a creative, restless mind. Here, everything needed to create the products was under one roof. Jack thrived in this opportunity to interact with all aspects of the business from production, artistic design, the written word, and marketing in order to create successful products.

In 1983 Jack was ready for a new challenge. He took his imagination, passion for teamwork, and marketing skills to Europe to develop a line of gifts and collectibles to complement Swarovski's award-winning crystal designs. Once again, his language skills were an advantage as in the role of *Hurricane Jack* he flew around Europe gathering a network of amazing artists, designers, and technicians to create beautiful objects in porcelain, wood, and silver.

Meanwhile, back in Kansas City, Jim Stowers, the Jonathan's neighbor, was experiencing the rapid expansion of his investment company, American Century Investments, that in the mid '80's had been recognized as having the best mutual funds in the country. The time had come to focus on the direct marketing and communication divisions of the company.

In 1988, Jim asked Jack to join the company and apply his innovative thinking to the direct marketing and communication divisions of the company. Wanting to help his investors understand the value of money and the importance of investing for the long term, Jim and Jack collaborated on creating a book, *Yes, You Can... Achieve Financial Independence.* This award-winning book broke new ground by using over 90 humorous illustrations.

In order to publish and market the book, Jack drew on his experience in publishing to set up a small company, Stowers Innovations, as a wholly owned subsidiary of American Century Investments. Over thirteen years of its existence, Stowers Innovations focused on helping people to achieve financial security. Besides their seven books, the team produced a quarterly newsletter, gave lectures, and reached out to the community via radio, television, and the Internet, all in an attempt to share Jim Stowers' hard-earned wisdom and philosophy about how to become financially independent.

In 1989, after Jim had recovered from the trauma of cancer, he and his wife were determined to create a research institute to help others who were suffering from life threatening diseases. Their dream began around the Stowers' kitchen table in the early '90s after Virginia had recovered from cancer. They invited over a few friends and colleagues, including Jack, to listen to their dream of finding a cure for cancer. By 1993, this Kitchen Cabinet had grown to include scientists and others with the knowledge needed to create a cutting-edge basic research institute focusing on gene-based diseases.

Throughout the six or seven years of planning and building the Stowers Institute for Medical Research, Jack, also a cancer survivor, was by Jim's side helping him write position papers, and vision and mission statements. He attended many of the meetings set up to organize and create the Stowers Institute for Medical Research. When the time came to build the center on the site of the Menorah Hospital campus, he played an active role: taking part in meetings to discuss fund raising and organizational issues, helping to write the prospectus for Jim's Hope Shares concept, and commissioning an artist to create the Institute's signature Hope for Life statue.

Jack was Jim's archivist, carefully keeping all the documents dealing with the history of this amazing undertaking. It was natural, then, that when Jim wanted someone to tell the story about how he and Virginia had created the Institute, he would turn to his longtime friend and co-author, Jack Jonathan. The manuscript was completed in the fall of 2011 and handed over to the Institute.

Larry Young's graceful thirty-one foot helix sculpture towers in front of the Stowers Institute for Medical Research. His statue, called *Hope for Life*, symbolizes how the secrets of life and health are embraced in the double helix that is our DNA.

Photography: an Avocation and Philanthropy

One of Jack's favorite quotes is: "It takes a long time to grow young." Now in his ninth decade, he could have followed convention and retired. But this was not for him. All his life he had worked diligently to help others succeed. Jack and Rena had always been generous in supporting community projects they believed in. Now, however, with time to focus on his art, Jack wanted to use his talent as an artist to give back to others.

He had a good team in place, and together, they brainstormed a new direction. Many projects were considered. Finally, they agreed that this last lap in the relay race of his life would be a focus on his photograph as philanthropy.

The first project of Jonathan & Associates was an installation at Children's Mercy Hospital that had just opened a new wing dedicated to Elisabeth Hall, beloved wife of Jack's mentor, Joyce Hall, founder of Hallmark Cards. A team of therapists from Children's Mercy Hospital was assembled to select 19 of Jack's color photographs that met his criterion of "healing images." The installation, *Healing Images*, is now permanently installed along the hallway leading to the new wing and in some of the treatment and examining rooms.

Hoping to have a retrospective of his 1952 exhibition in Cairo, Jack then turned the attention of his team to that venture. Archival material was sorted and catalogued, research on Egypt was gathered, a selection of the 90 images for an exhibition *Egypt, the Eternal Spirit of Its People*, were chosen, digitized and framed. Soon the office became a mini-gallery of wonderful images of the people in and around Cairo in the 1950's. Finally, Molly Proffer created a public relations DVD of Jack and his exhibition.

2013 Photograph by Greg Miloto

The dream has become reality. Jack in his studio surrounded by four images of his exhibition.

The project got a big boost when Molly and her son Ben introduced Jack to an Egyptian reporter, Hanan El Badry. Stepping into Jack's office, Hanan was astonished by what she saw. There, emanating from the walls of the gallery was the warmth and beauty of her country in scenes of lives lived before she was born. Overcome with excitement, she sent the Proffer's DVD to Dr. Ismail Serageldin, head of the Bibliotheca Alexandrina in Alexandria, Egypt. Now, it was Jack's turn to be surprised when unexpectedly, Dr. Serageldin phoned and declared, "We need these pictures in Egypt." With that statement, Jack's dream of mounting a retrospective of his 1952 exhibition suddenly became a reality.

The January 15, 2016 opening of the exhibition, *Egypt, the Eternal Spirit of Its People*, at the Bibliotheca Alexandrina will be a highlight of Jack's life. But he does not intend it to be his Swan Song. His passion for photography draws him forward. In production already are several new projects that will enable him to continue to use his photography to help other people.

"Jack Jonathan's riveting photographs give us a glimpse of Egypt that is as fresh and revealing today as it was more than half a century ago."

Bruce Bradley, History of Science Librarian (retired)
Linda Hall Library, Kansas City, Missouri

PART II

Egypt

The Eternal Spirit of Its People

Stories of an Exhibition

Egypt, The Eternal Spirit of Its People:
Stories of an Exhibition

The Story Continues...

A Retrospective Exhibition, 2016 48

Introduction: **Seeing Into The Heart of Things** 50

Egypt's Timeless Environment

Egypt's Timeless Environment 53

Land of the Pharaohs 54

Strolling Through Old Cairo 62

The Eternal Spirit of the People

Faces of Old Cairo 74

Egypt – The Gift of the Nile 91

The Land and Its People 113

A Glimpse of Bedouin Life 142

Biographies of My Team 160

The Story Continues...

A Retrospective Exhibition, 2016

Working in my dark room in Cairo using a traditional chemical printing process, I was able to create extraordinary black and white prints for my 1952 exhibition, *Scenes of Egypt.*

Years later the advent of digital photography and inkjet printing motivated me to apply this new technology to recreate the exhibition. With the help of Steve Barr, the negatives were digitized and given new life when printed with an inkjet printer. I believe that the artistic value of my work has been enhanced because the digital process reveals details and contrasts that were not possible before.

A Fulbright scholar, Will Masters, attended the original opening in 1952 and wrote a scholarly, glowing critique of the show. He ended with a quote from a 19th C French artist, Odilon Redon, that he felt fit my exhibition, "Black is the most essential of all colors. Black is the photographer's medium and the skill, the patience, and the artistic sense necessary to exploit it are in the extreme."

My fascination with the play of light and shadow could have been rendered in color. However, using only shades of black, my photography has a three-dimensional quality that is more intimate and emotionally appealing, inviting the viewer to make a personal interpretation of the photograph.

Sixty-four years after my exhibitions in Egypt, my dream to show these images again has been unexpectedly fulfilled. A chance introduction to Dr. Ismail Serageldin, director of the Bibliotheca Alexandrina, led to an exhibition, *Egypt, The Eternal Spirit of Its People*, in Alexandria, Egypt, January 15, 2016. Other exhibitions are being planned.

Perhaps these images of the kind and hospitable people living around Cairo will serve as an inspiration in this time of violence in the Middle East. At the very least, I hope these photographs can help us understand this ancient land and its resilient people.

*"Black is the most essential of all colors.
Black is the photographer's medium
and the skill, the patience,
and the artistic sense necessary
to exploit it are in the extreme."*

Odilon Redon

Seeing Into The Heart of Things

What a colorful, cosmopolitan chaos Cairo was in the 1920's and '30's when I was a boy. On the weekends we might walk to the market with our father. How delicious it was to smell peanuts roasting, to buy sweet potatoes, to taste the tamarind juice. How fascinated we were to watch the shoemaker mending sandals or watch a man and his son working a lathe. How proud we were to walk home, single file, each with a watermelon of the perfect size atop our heads.

Early in the 1930's we moved to a farming community east of Cairo called Ezbet el Nakhl (Village of the Date Palms). We played along the canal and in the sugar cane fields. There was plenty of work on a dairy farm for us children. One memory I cherish was getting up at sunrise to help Bayoumi, our stalwart Nubian farmhand, milk our water buffalo herd before we boarded the train to an Italian school in Cairo. During school vacation I was often assigned to sit on a little cart, sleepy in the sun, occasionally cracking a whip to urge my water buffalo to go round and round to winnow the wheat.

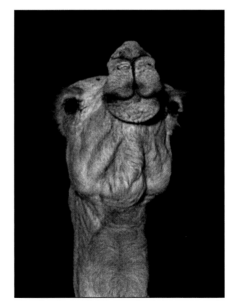

Later, as a young man, I loved to ride in the desert before sunrise, reveling in the sound of the horse's hooves breaking the crust off the dew-laden sand. Sometimes, on those rides I enjoyed the hospitality of the Bedouins and endured the scrutiny of their grumpy camels.

I have always looked into the heart of things. When I bought my first camera, my desire was to reveal the inner beauty of a person or scene. My photographs recorded unrehearsed moments in the lives of ordinary people living in the wonderful land of my birth.

When I selected photographs for my first exhibition in 1952, I wanted to show this fascinating, ancient country at its best – to capture the spirit of the Egyptians who went about their daily life much as their ancestors had. My sensitivity for the land and its people enabled me to create a series of images that are warm and intimate.

This was a chaotic time, with a worldwide financial crisis that affected everyone. Nevertheless, there was also a wonderful atmosphere of harmony in Cairo because people treated each other with acceptance, respect, and civility. I did not want my photographs to dwell on the poverty and hardships that were obvious. I wanted to capture the dignity and quiet joy with which these hard-working people faced their daily challenges.

Tourists look for an adventure. What they will experience is the vastness and solitude of the desert.

This picture was featured in an article in *The Coronet*, June 1953, that described the scene this way:

...Here, on the edge of vastness, eternity is one's neighbor; here man and beast move together, figures on a landscape old as time...

Waiting for Riders

6

Egypt's Timeless Environment

Growing up in Cairo, the pyramids were a symbol of power connected with the Old Testament. Passing through the ancient gates of Cairo and walking by the many lovely mosques, the ambience of antiquity was simply a part of the environment.

Later, as a young man, I was caught up in the excitement of the city with its diverse cultures. Not until I was earning a living and was able to ride into the desert did I really appreciate how the desert and the river and the history of my homeland were a deep part of me.

I became conscious of the way the sun rose over the desert; of the moods of the old Cairo gates and mosques as the sun crossed over them during the day, highlighting the nooks and crannies. My first chance to record my feelings of intimacy with this environment was after I learned to use a camera. When the lens framed an intricate window in the mosque, I was drawn to its beauty. When the immensity of the pyramids overwhelmed me, I focused on the details of those great structures, seeing them in ways often not captured before.

I present here photographs of the most ancient monuments and some of the historic architecture of Cairo. It is my hope that the viewer can feel the sense of history that pervades the lives of each Egyptian.

Land of the Pharaohs

Still a mystery after centuries of probing and speculation, the pyramids and the Sphinx are the first images that come to mind when one thinks of Egypt, whose history is intimately tied with these ancient monuments.

For millennia the Sphinx has been a silent witness to each passing civilization. Walking up to the Sphinx, one has the sense of being scrutinized by a being from the ancient past. To stand below the impressive head of the Sphinx is overwhelming and awe-inspiring.

I was content just to admire and photograph these antiquities, hoping to capture the mood of greatness I experienced in the solitude of my early morning rides in the desert.

An Eternal Presence

A Wish for Long Life

The United States Ambassador to Cairo, Jefferson Caffery, enjoyed mountain climbing. Having been in France for four years, he missed his favorite sport. Often on the weekends he would drive to the pyramids of Giza where he would challenge the local guide in a race to the top.

My friend, Robert Simpson, the Ambassador's personal secretary, would invite me to tag along. While the Ambassador was busy climbing, the director of the archeological digs in the area would invite us to view the latest discovery.

On one trip, I brought my camera and had the good fortune to be there as the newly uncovered temple doorways were brought out of the sand after over 3,000 years. I was able to capture this unique image through the doorways of the temple showing the well-preserved bas-relief on the right side of the doorframe.

The following morning, when the Ambassador saw the prints, he immediately called the Director of Egyptian Antiquities at the Egyptian Museum of Antiquities in Cairo, a French Abbot named Abbé Drioton, (since the time of Napoleon's ill-fated conquest of Egypt in 1798, this post was traditionally administered by a French archeologist.

Ambassador Caffery standing in the doorways examining the bas-relief.

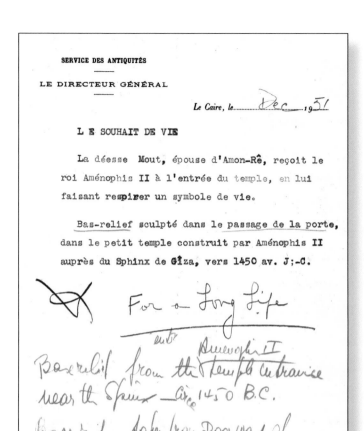

With my photograph in hand, I was sent to talk to Abbé Drioton and discover the meaning of the bas-relief.

As I explained the circumstances of how I took the photograph, Abbé Drioton, without consulting any texts, quickly typed the meaning of the greeting in French.

The Goddess Mout, wife of Amon Re,
greets the King Amenophis the II,
at the entrance of the Temple by extending
to him the symbol of life. (Ankh).

Ambassador Caffery, amazed by the 3,000 year old symbolic gesture to celebrate life, asked me to adapt the bas-relief photograph to create a Christmas card with the following wish: "For a Long Life."

Perhaps this was a sign of things to come, as only a few years later I would begin a thirty-year career with Hallmark Cards.

For a Long Life Christmas 1951

East of the Sphinx lie
the remnants of an old
temple dedicated to
King Amenophis
II (circa 1450 BCE).
On the right frame
of the temple doors a
bas-relief shows the
Goddess Mout greeting
King Amenophis II with
an ankh – the key of life
and a sign of
prosperity and health.

For a Long Life

2

Doorways to the Riddle

3

These doorways were
moved to the Egyptian
Museum of Antiquities
in Cairo shortly after
being discovered in1951.

"From the Gate of Amenophis Temple, the daughter of the 20th C stands reading a glorious page from our history expressed on the silent face of the Sphinx."

Quoted from *Al Mussawar* weekly journal, a critique of my 1952 exhibition in Cairo.

The Beauty and the Sphinx

3

Tourists by the Great Pyramid

This photograph dramatizes the contrast between the scale of the people and the majestic dimensions of the pyramid.

5

Strolling Through Old Cairo

Like its mother country, Cairo itself has layers of history, as thirty-five generations of leaders ruled the area, naming their capitals Memphis, Heliopolis, Babylon-in-Egypt, Al-Fustat, Al-Qataei, or Al-Askar. Finally, in 969 CE, the Muslims built a city on the site of modern Cairo and named it Al-Qahira, *The Triumphant*. So ancient is the city, so central to the country, that Egyptians sometimes refer to Cairo as *Masr* suggesting that Cairo is equivalent to Egypt.

My first photographs of Cairo were taken in a walk around the old city with an historian, Gaston Wiet. We focused on the ancient walls and mosques of the area. The city walls and two gates of Cairo were built in 1092 CE. But it was the ruler Saladin who extended those fortifications between 1176 — 1183 CE in an attempt to protect the city from the crusaders. His intention was to unite Cairo and Fustat into one great city in the Citadel, built on a promontory beneath the Al-Muqattam Hills.

I was fascinated with the beautiful mosques with their many facets. The Muhammad Ali mosque stands out from the rest because it was built on the summit of the Citadel so it can be seen from all over Cairo. It was Muhammad Ali Pasha who, in 1805 CE, established the dynasty that brought Egypt into the modern era by embarking on a program of agricultural, administrative, and military reforms along European lines. His dynasty ended with the abdication of King Farouk and the dissolution of the monarchy in 1953.

These photographs of old Cairo focus on the way light and shadow create an almost mystical feeling about these extraordinary structures.

Leaving Cairo through Bab el-Foutouh Gate

Cairo: The City of a Thousand Minarets

A mosque was the legacy of many rulers. However, one of the most important mosques in Cairo, Al-Hakim Mosque (#12), was named in honor of an Imam. It was built in 990 CE using a similar design to the mosque attached to the Al-Azhar University, built 20 years earlier.

One of my favorite photographic subjects was the Khayrbak Mosque (#13), built in 1520 CE by the first Ottoman governor of Egypt. Typical of many mosques, it had a dual purpose as a gathering shelter for prayer and as a religious school (madrassa). I loved the many aspects of its minaret and dome that loomed over the surrounding structures.

The Citadel is so crowded that one mosque may cast a shadow on the wall of another. I was fortunate to arrive at the Al-Rifa'i Mosque in time to capture a stunning image (#11). The Sultan Hassan Mosque cast a shadow high upon the wall of the Al-Rifa'i Mosque and my eyes were drawn to the intricate crenulations and delicate carvings.

Undoubtedly the star of the show is the overpowering Muhammad Ali Mosque, which was inaugurated in 1848. Slender and elegant when viewed from a distance, it looms high and massive close up and has a unique feature – two minarets. Designed by Yusuf Bushnak of Istanbul in the style of the Ottomans, it is paradoxically a symbol of strength and delicacy as seen in the window detail of photograph #9.

The tomb of Muhammad Ali is housed in the sheltered courtyard (# 8), whose porticoes isolate the worshippers from the distractions of city life. The beauty of the mosque inspires peace, contemplation, and a focus on the divine. Even today, it is an oasis of peace in the middle of the chaos that is Cairo.

Muhammad Ali Mosque Courtyard – An oasis of peace

8

Muhammad Ali Mosque – Window Detail 9

Muhammad Ali Mosque

10

This photograph was featured on the cover of the catalogue of my 1952 exhibition, *Scenes of Egypt,* in Cairo and Alexandria.

Minaret of the Al-Rifa'i Mosque　　　　　　　　　11

Minaret of Al-Hakim Mosque

12

Khayrbak Mosque

13

"People of the Book" Living in Harmony

A Coptic Church, a Jewish Temple, and the Muhammad Ali Mosque evoke Cairo's historic legacy as a cultural and religious crossroads.

14

The Eternal Spirit of the People of Egypt

The pyramids, the Nile, and the feluccas are the three symbols most central to the eternal spirit of Egypt. The Nile is the source of life in this ancient land; the feluccas are sailing boats essential for the transportation and communication that supported the country's prosperity. The pyramids represent Egypt's enduring culture.

Growing up in Egypt, I encountered people of vastly different cultures, yet they were alike in their spirit of warmth, hospitality, and humor. Preparing for my *Scenes of Egypt* exhibition in 1952, I wanted to reconnect with the people and experiences of my childhood, so I focused on life in and around Cairo. I was particularly drawn to the country folk whose lives unfolded in the slow rhythms of tradition; people who relied on the river, or the rich land of the Delta for their livelihood. My love of horses and the desert had given me a feeling of empathy with the Bedouin.

Looking at these people with 21st century eyes, you may think that they lived in poverty. However, they had enough food, a place to live, adequate clothing, and above all a supportive community. I felt a deep connection to these people whose simple lives were lived with a sense of self-confident richness, contentment, and hope for the future.

Enough is as good as a feast when you do not compare yourself with others, as this bit of Arabian wisdom suggests:

"الغنى: قلة تمنيك، و الرضا بما يكفيك"

"Wealth: wishing for little and contentment with what is sufficient."

Collected from
KnightsofArabia.com
by Aisha Bilal

Symbols of Egypt's Eternal Vigor

Felucca's do not commonly cluster so closely together. Here, they sailed as a group because the bridge had just opened. Though the pyramids appear close to the Nile, they are at least eight miles from it.

15

Faces of Old Cairo

Egypt's history is an unending parade of conquest and foreign domination. Yet in the end, these outsiders are absorbed into the national character of Egypt. In this way, the spirit of Egypt is, indeed, eternal. People of all levels of the society are unified in a temperament that includes an innate sense of courtesy and hospitality, a love of children, and a veneration of old age.

Cairo had a fascinating mix of people. I could have focused on the blue-clad porters, or the white-clad policemen, or the many foreigners who called Egypt home. But it was the ordinary Cairenes who fascinated me. I captured these images while strolling through overcrowded colorful neighborhoods that have evolved over many centuries.

In the old Cairo neighborhoods there was an abundance of variety. These are but a few: an elegant Muslim woman wearing her veil as a fashion statement; an older woman dressed traditionally in black; sidewalk artisans; strolling vendors; school children learning to read; a religious scholar and a professor.

They evoke Cairo's legacy as an ethnic melting pot of ancient and modern traditions, a conglomerate of diverse cultural enclaves.

This photograph
illustrates the
diversity of people
crowding into the old
city on a typical day.

Entering Old Cairo through the Bab el-Foutouh Gate   16

Education   *"Love letters as thy mother"*

ancient Egyptian maxim

Egyptian culture has always valued education as the bridge to the future. As far back as the Old Kingdom, the life of a scribe was considered an ideal life according to the *Instructions of Ptah-hotep.* Nearly 2000 years later, in 288 BCE, Egyptian influence in worldwide scholarship was greatly enhanced with the founding of the great Library of Alexandria, the "Lighthouse to the World." Continuing with the tradition of scholarship, the great university of Cairo, Al-Azhar, was founded as a madrassa in 972 CE. It is now one of the oldest degree-granting universities in the world.

During my time in Egypt, there was a nationalistic fervor to create a rebirth in the country by educating all children. The many public primary schools tried to catch up with the ever-increasing demand. There were many excellent private schools established for the multicultural population: English, French, Italian, and Greek were some of them.

There was a social center near the Citadel that had a library (#17), and the USIS in Cairo had a reading room (#27) and library.

I took this picture in 1949 for a book titled *The Art of Libraries in Service of the Youth*, by Fan Al Maktabat and Fi Khedmet Al Nash.

The Legacy of the Past – The Promise of the Future   17

Allah Illalah   18

An alim (scholar) reading his Koran, waiting
for the muezzin to call the faithful to prayer.

Learning to Love Books   19

Learning English at the USIS reading room in Cairo.

The Souk – Market

Cairo, the city of contrasts, was a photographer's paradise. Passing through the crowded neighborhoods, one could experience the very special mix of unique individuals who shared the same language and customs with foreigners who called Cairo home (#20).

This souk featured permanent shops with display spaces inside and out. A merchant might rent space in front of his business to vendors with moveable carts. Sometimes, the shopkeeper himself would have a moveable display that he rolled in at night and secured behind a gate of aluminum (#21).

People traded and lived in these old neighborhoods where space was at a premium. A shopkeeper's family might live in an apartment above the store.

Instead of renting space in front of a shop, street-vendors might move their cart from site to site to entice customers with their wares. Corn on the cob (#22), sweet potatoes (#23), tamarind juice – these are a few of the delicious treats available from the street vendors.

The sidewalks in the Souk were the ateliers for artisans who created beautiful art (#25), or mended shoes, or worked a lathe (#24), while sitting cross-legged on a small space on the pavement.

Sharia Al-Arabiah – Gateway to the Souk 20

A Souk in Old Cairo   The vendor sold cold tamarind juice (tamar hindi, Indian date)   21
with choices of lime or honey in it.

Students from the school gather around the corn vendor eagerly waiting to sink their teeth into the tender, juicy corn.

Corn on the Cob

22

Coming down from the Citadel one evening at dusk, we looked back at the impressive, looming presence of the Muhammad Ali Mosque. As we stood in awed silence, a sweet potato vendor passed by. His presence intensified a magic moment, dramatizing the contrast between daily life and sacred tradition.

Sweet Potato Vendor   23

Foot Powered Lathe 24

The young apprentice is
the craftsman's son.

Silversmith 25

The silversmith practices
an old art form, repoussé.

Passing Strangers, Deep in Thought   26

Although this street is in the heart of the old city near the Citadel, it is uncharacteristically quiet. The whole scene speaks to us in symbols.

The weathered stones of the thousand-year old wall are striking next to the modern gas lamp. The play of light and shadow on the wall creates an otherworldly feeling.

Two strangers seemingly unaware of each other, silently pass, lost in their own thoughts.

Contagious Laughter 27

I was lucky to have my camera available to capture this gentleman's spontaneous laugh. He was a professor who often visited the library at the Embassy. We greeted each other and exchanged jokes. When he burst into laughter, I laughed with him.

His dazzling smile shows the contrast between his perfect white teeth and his fine unblemished dark skin.

Tradition: The Fashionable Choice 28

Welcoming Smile   29

The Nubians in Cairo were faithful,
honest, hard-working people. This man
was a janitor in a public building. His
lovely white teeth may have been a
bonus from his habit of enjoying the treat
of chewing on sugar cane which doubles
as a toothbrush. His welcoming smile
reminded me of my friend, Bayoumi,
who worked on our dairy farm.

Reserved Welcome   30

Groppi, The Place to Be Seen in 1951

Here in the heart of Cairo, wide streets were lined with beautiful buildings. There was a throb of energy and a sense of purpose from the steady stream of cars and the bustle of people. Yet, only a few blocks away, Cairo took back its old cloak.

In 1951, my wife and I would take our evening stroll down the street where we lived, up to the square, past the statue and down Talaat Harb to Groppi, a Swiss pâtisserie. There, foreigners sat side by side with Cairenes, savoring small cups of strong coffee, and delighting in sweet confections. My wife favored the marrons glacés and I enjoyed sipping an espresso while smoking my pipe.

This was the favorite place to be, where people gathered to talk about the news of the day.

Traffic Circle, now Mostafa Kamel Square 31

"Hail to thee O Nile!
Who manifests thyself
in this land,
and comes to give
life to Egypt."

From "Hymn to the Nile" circa 2100 BCE

Egypt– The Gift of the Nile

What is the secret of Egypt? Why is it one of the oldest continuous civilizations in the world? For over 5000 years foreigners who coveted the wealth of the country invaded it. However, the spirit of Egypt is so pervasive that to live in that great nation is to become a part of it.

Egypt was the envy of the civilized ancient world because of the great river that flowed along its length, endowing the region with wealth that in turn created unity and constancy. The great annual floods of this watery gift were the most important natural cycles of the calendar, cycles that were embedded in the Egyptian psyche. So critical were the floods to the people's survival that the Pharaohs allied themselves with the High Priests to control the wealth that accrued from this phenomenon.

Knowledge is Power

In ancient Egypt, the Pharaoh ruled with absolute power tempered only by the high priests. Together, they used the science of the day to predict and control the outcome of crucial events. One of the primary bases of their power was their ability to accurately predict the annual flooding of the Nile.

The fertile banks and delta of the Nile depended on the annual inundation and its deposit of silt. Nilometers, descending staircases leading down into the river, were used to measure the depth of the rising water over the last 1000 miles upstream. These measurements, recorded over decades, enabled the priests to predict the amount of floodwater that could be expected. A good flood would mean bountiful silt and good crops; in those years, the Pharaoh could increase taxes. A prediction of a dry year would prompt the priests to consider the amount of offerings they needed to "pacify" the Nile god Hapi. So the elite had it both ways, whether there was a drought or a flood, the offerings or taxes would fill the coffers of the Pharaoh and the high priests.

The Nile Celebration: Wafaa El-Nil

August 15th marked the beginning of the ancient Egyptian calendar – the season of Akhet, the inundation. A ritual was held to honor the god of the Nile, Hapi, to invoke him to bring fertility to the land. A maiden used to be sacrificed to this Nile god. When I was a boy, a sugar maiden was thrown into the river.

In my time this was not a religious rite; it was a celebration of life. Boats on the river were hung with streamers and crowded with people leaning over the side. On the shore, people milled around. Some women sheltered under umbrellas to protect themselves from the relentless heat of the sun (#34). A group of fortunate children had a choice view from atop their parents' shoulders (#33).

Mixing in among the celebrants were vendors: an old man with an armful of paper hats (#32); a man selling balloons; a vendor selling paper cones of roasted melon seeds (#34).

It was a great celebration enjoyed by people of every station in life.

Wafaa El-Nil, Nile Celebration   32

Above the Crowd, a Choice View   33

Nile Celebration – Savoring Melon Seeds   34

Irrigation

Egyptians devised ways to benefit from the annual flooding of the Nile from July through December. Canals were dug along the Nile to divert the floods and silt, and to expand the reach of the water onto the fields. Because the canals were lower than the fields, the water had to be lifted up and over the banks onto the land. I photographed three different irrigation techniques.

The oldest method was a *bucket brigade* (#35). In this photograph fellaheen on one side of the canal use this ancient method, while on the other bank a shadouf is used (#37).

A *shadouf* operates on the principles of physics. A pole is balanced on a cross beam with a rope and bucket on one end and a heavy weight on the other. The bucket is swung out over the bank and lowered into the river. When the operator pushes down on the counter weight, he can raise the bucket full of water, swing it around, and empty it into the field or a small canal.

Archimedes invented the *tambour* when he paid a visit to Egypt circa 250 BCE. It is a screw inside a hollow tube. When the screw is turned, the bottom end of the screw rotates and lifts the water along the tube to the top (#36).

Catching Catfish

Every year the irrigation canal that bordered our farm was drained and dredged. When the water was only one-foot deep, the catfish could be caught by hand. All the neighborhood kids would come out to harvest the fish. It was a great celebration.

Irrigation by Bucket Brigade   35

Irrigation by Tambour
(Archimedes Screw, circa 250 BCE)

36

Irrigation by Shadouf (circa 1700 BCE)

37

Harvesting the Nile

The Egyptian fisherman exists between the water, the sky, and God (#38).

In my time, there were many kinds of fish in the river: catfish, tilapia, eels, moonfish and puffer fish, to name a few. In fact, there was such an abundance of fish that the water was crowded with boats. A man could sell his daily catch to local hotels and restaurants and still have enough fish to feed his family.

A fisherman would weave and repair his own linen and cotton nets (#39). When he was out fishing, sometimes for days at a time, his boat was his home. Here he slept, and cooked and ate his meals of pita and ful mudammes (fava beans) washed down with cups of mint tea (#40).

Traditionally, a son would inherit the father's boat and livelihood. Even in challenging years, a fisherman was reluctant to trade his vocation, because the Nile gave him everything he needed.
It was a challenging but good life.

InSha'Allah: God Willing   A silent prayer that, InSha'Allah, the nets will be full.   38

Mending Nets 39

Time Out for Lunch   40

Feluccas, the Trucks of the Nile

The Nile and the irrigation canals are a blessing to Egypt not only because of the irrigation benefits, but because they establish a waterway system the length of Egypt – from the first cataract to the rich Delta. The feluccas can carry enormous quantities of non-perishable goods; for example, an obelisk. Imagine the strength and balance required to carry such a huge monolith.

Egypt gave obelisks to France, England, and the United States. All came by felucca from the quarries in the south near the first cataract, up to Alexandria where they were loaded onto seagoing vessels whose prows had to be modified to accommodate the lengthy cargo.

Now, a thirty-foot felucca may carry limestone from the quarries up river to near the first Nile cataract. A felucca rides very low in the water when it is fully loaded (#41).

It takes a great deal of skill to sail a felucca because of its large triangular sail that is designed to be its main source of power. However, when the wind is down a craft is laboriously moved by poling. The sailor projects a long pole into the river bed and pulls it toward him as he walks from bow to stern. Another sailor stands at the stern and mans the outboard tiller (#46).

There are many levels of men working on these beautifully designed vessels, sailors (#45), captains (#44) and felucca fleet owners (#42). They perform a variety of tasks: such as poling, setting the sails, loading the feluccas, mending the sails. I never saw the person who baked the pita and laid it out on the deck of the felucca to dry in the sun (#48).

Loaded Felucca

Fleet Owner   A confident smile from the successful fleet owner.   42

Adjusting the Sails 43

Felucca Captain (Rais)   44

Young Sailor   45

Manpower

Nile Transport Fleet   47

Our Daily Aish (Pita)

48

Felucca Contrejour

The Land and Its People

Rural life is difficult in every country, and Egyptian rural life was no exception. In my time, seventy-five percent of Egyptians were engaged in farming, a lifestyle that entailed long hours of labor. The fellaheen lived in houses built of unfired mud bricks. Their villages clustered along the river and canals that brought them life and prosperity.

When I captured these images in 1952, young women still carried water from the wells and wheat was threshed laboriously by a water buffalo walking slowly around in a circle. Farm equipment was simple, non-mechanical, and guided or driven by human or animal energy.

Yet, there was a sense of timelessness and harmony in the simple, hard-working life of the fellaheen (peasants). The people seemed not just content, but happy and joyful.

A Village Prospering by the Nile   50

Rowing Across

This man's main source of income is ferrying
people across the Nile from their village.

51

My Innocent Gamousa Calf

When I was ten years old my family moved to a village called Ezbet el-Nakhl where my Dad, an agronomist, dreamed of practicing his profession. Our farm was named Dairy Myra after my newborn sister.

From our herd of one hundred water buffalo, my father selected a bull calf for me to raise. Like any pet, he followed me around and when he was old enough. I played toreador with him in the corral.

I did not realize how much he had grown. One afternoon, as I teased him with my red cloth, he came after me. I jumped the fence, but to my horror, he jumped after me.

I ran like a scared rabbit down the alley of date palms looking for one I could climb. With bare feet, and clad only in shorts, I scrambled up the most suitable one.

My thighs and feet were spotted with blood from the prickly bark. I looked down in awe and amazement at the snorting, pawing, not so innocent, bull calf.

The Irreplaceable Gamousa

The gamousa was the workhorse of rural Egypt, performing a variety of services for the farmers. Our dairy farm got its milk from the gamousa. But the gamousa was also used in place of a tractor to bring in the hay (#53) or plow the fields.

One of my jobs on the farm was to thresh the grain. I would sit on a little bench and crack my whip to make the gamousa pull the threshing platform endlessly around the circle of grain (#54).

Gamousa Calf   52

Making Hay

Threshing the Grain   Sitting in the hot sun, endlessly going around in a circle,   54
the boys may have been tempted to daydream.

Riding High on Her Trusty Gamousa

55

Watering Gamousas   Gamousas, like other animals, do not drink stagnant water. Here, they   56
                         are standing in the fresh flowing water of the Nile to quench their thirst.

Transportation in the Countryside

Many animals are pressed into service as vehicles for the transport of humans and produce: camels, horses, donkeys, gamousas. Often, the humans, especially the women, walk. Tradition in the country ruled that the man rode in front while the woman walked a respectful distance behind (#57).

If it were not for the telegraph poles we might think this was a scene from biblical times.

Trail of Flour

These pictures remind me of my life on the farm, when, riding high on a lumpy saddle of grain, I would take our wheat to the flourmill a quarter of a mile from our farm. Coming home was a pleasure, as the "saddle" was now a cushion of soft, milled flour. One day, lulled by the hot sun into a pleasant daydream, I seemed to be gently floating. By the time I got home, there was a trail of flour all along the road where it had escaped from a small hole in the sack.

A Country Life Tradition   Two donkeys, two people, yet only one rides.   57

More Than a Ship of the Desert   58

Reliable Transportation   59

This burro is loaded with clover that is used
for animal fodder.

Quadriped Taxi   60

The whole family rides in style.

Bedouin Friend   61

A burro is a blessing to the
poor everywhere.

Fellah of Tomorrow – A Future Beyond the Faas

The Rural Village

Everything the fellaheen needed was found in the village – many people never went beyond the village walls or fields. Here they worked, married, raised children, played games, grew their food, and worshipped. Rural parents were very attentive to their children who were an integral part of the village and its future. From an early age they were expected to take responsibilities at home and in the community. They fed and cared for the geese (#67) and other small animals; the girls carried water from the well or the river (#66); and the older children looked after the younger ones.

In a time before television, and even radio, there was still plenty of time for school and recreation. But the rhythm of village life circled around religious obligations and celebrations. A man or woman who had fulfilled the holy duty of all good Muslims and gone on a pilgrimage to Meccah would be treated with great respect in the village (#72).

In the spring of 1952 I was in Quasim village with Father Ayrout, who wrote the well-known book The Fellah. I searched all day for an Egyptian youth who embodied the strength and potential of Egypt's future. I had almost given up hope when I saw this young boy – handsome, determined, and healthy – the perfect subject. He was preparing to leave for home after a day in the field that began at sunrise. His evening would be full of studying, for not only does he feel the responsibility for his family, but also for a future beyond the faas.

Village Child   63

Her days are still carefree.

Universal Fascination with New Life   64

After the eggs hatched, the fellaheen brought the chicks to this
special clay enclosure to protect them while they grew.

Wash Day 65

It is easier to wash the clothes in the canal
than bring the water to the house.

Back from the Well 66

Everything seems like an adventure when you are young.

Chasing Runaway Ducks 67

Watching the family geese?
Or playing a game?
Any way you look at it,
this child was having fun.

This little boy was holding tight, feeling safe in the sheltering arms of his dad.

Father and Son at Home

68

Rural Life – Adults

The women seemed to make their many tasks light by enjoying each other's company. When the Singer Sewing Machine Company made it possible for even a small village to have a sewing machine on a lend/lease basis, the women gathered around the machine for conversation as well as work (#74).

Women in traditional cultures are the carriers of all things. They begin young when they carry heavy pots of water back from the well or the river (#66). You see elegance in motion when a woman carries her market purchases on her head, hands free, head high (#75).

I experienced these hard-working rural women as open-hearted and joyful. They seemed delighted when I spoke to them in their own language. One woman in particular laughed heartily (#69) when I greeted her with a common Arabic greeting, "May your morning be like cream."

The life of the fellaheen followed the slow natural rhythms of the sun. They rose at dawn and worked until the sun set. The center of their lives was faith, family, and the community. Contentment rested in this simplicity, for usually, what they had was enough and life was good.

Sabah al-Ishta: "May your morning be like cream." 69

This woman burst into hearty laughter at my unexpected Arabic greeting.

School Recess Soccer Game   Soccer, the national sport in Egypt, was played on every available open space.   70

Nabbout Jousting – Ancient Pastime

Jousting with a heavy stick (nabbout) 71
is a pastime as old as the Crusades.

El-Hajj – The Village Elder   This man has fulfilled his duty by going on a pilgrimage (Haj) to Mecca.   72

Delta Fellah 73

Singer Sewing Circle   The sewing circle is an opportunity to share stories and gossip.   74

Hands-Free, an Elegant Posture

A natural elegance with her head high and her hands free.

75

Dates: The Fruit of Light

Date palm trees are everywhere in Egypt. The fruit grows in long strands that form into bunches near the top of the trees. A bunch is harvested before all the dates are ripe and appetizing.

These trees were a wonderful part of my childhood on the farm. Between September and December when the dates were ready to harvest, my Dad would cut a bunch and hang it on the breezeway between our house and one of the outbuildings.

"... the fruit of the date is 'three skies above luxury.' and as indispensable as water and air..."

from *Date Palm Trinity*, by Khaled Mattawa

When we left the house, we would carefully choose a perfectly ripe date to munch. Grasping the stem, we would gently squeeze the date until the soft inner flesh squirted into our mouths leaving the skin between our fingers. Our tongue would move the fruit around until the pit was in front and then we could spit it out onto the sand.

Date palms hold a treasure, but they don't provide the fun that mango trees do. Our farm was edged with towering mango trees. One of our great adventures was to climb those trees with an indelible pencil firmly clenched in our teeth. We would select a few choice green mangoes, wet the tip of the pencil, and carefully write our initials on the fruit. While they were ripening, we would run out to the trees to check on our mangoes. What fun it was to watch our initials slowly stretch across the growing fruit. Woe to the sibling who plucked a coveted mango not his own!

Food for the Body and Soul

76

A Glimpse of Bedouin Life

The desert has a strange hold on its people. The magical solitude, the scorching heat of the day, and the cold eroding winds of the night, has bred a unique individual. The Bedouin are proud of their ability to survive in an environment that others see as hostile. For the Bedouin, the desert is a place of community – a vast community without fixed boundaries. What is fixed for the Bedouin, is their family, the center of their lives. Their sprawling tents house all the generations of one family. A collection of related families will form tribes that have elected tribal leaders (Sheikhs) who take responsibility for the well-being of their people (#82).

Although men and women of the family have very distinct roles, they are equal partners. Many of the Bedouin men are herders of goats, sheep, or camels. Some are breeders of the Arabian horses that are revered by the culture. The women are in charge of the tent, the children, and the tribe's generous hospitality that requires the accommodating of guests for up to three days. In my time, the women cooked their family's meals on an open fire. One weekly task was the baking of a supply of small thick loaves of flat bread (leba) made of wheat and barley (#79).

Bedouin people have fine features and a proud carriage like their ancestors. Often, the women will have tattoos on their faces to mark her tribal family (#83). I found Bedouin women to be more comfortable with my presence than women of Cairo. They seemed so self assured (#78, 80).

Halfway between El Alamein and Alexandria, a unique place was designed and built by an English army officer, W.J. Bramley. He loved the Bedouins and wanted to live among them, so in in the early 1900's, with the encouragement of the father of King Farouk, King Fouad, he built a little walled village, Borg el Arab. The walls of the Borg were made from white limestone quarried from the area of the old Roman aqueduct. After visiting the Borg, E.M. Forster wrote, "Bedouin don't build. But if they did, they would build a village like this one."

Because they do not like to be boxed-in, the Bedouin set up their tents outside the walls, and brought their animals into the courtyard to trade for staples like food and clothing. There were no roads to the village and it seemed lonely and isolated. Yet, people from all over the world were drawn to it. Some stayed on, some were guests, put up in the apartments in the Borg.

When I saw this lovely mother and child happy inside the family tent, I could not help but draw a parallel between this image and that of Fra Filippo Lippi's renaissance painting, *Madonna and Child With Two Angels*. How exquisite the delicate fingers of this baby resting on her mother's hand. How soft and secure the mother's embrace.

Bedouin Madonna

77

Bedouin Fashion   This young woman has an air of dignity and self-assurance.   78

Cooking the Morning Meal   79

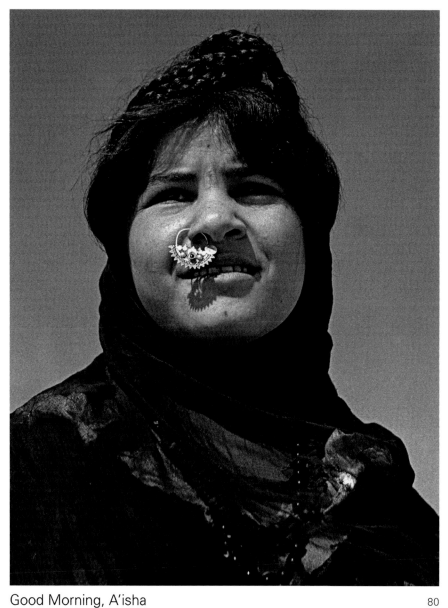

Good Morning, A'isha

80

There was an inner light shining from A'isha that eclipsed her golden nose ring.

Lazeeza – Sheikh's daughter

81

Seen in
Rollei Photography,
Jacob Deschin,
1952

Sheikh Muhammad – Dressed for Celebration

82

Moukhtar, an Egyptian
sculptor I met in 1952, said of
Egyptian women, "She fights
an everlasting battle against
disease, poverty and sorrow.
Yet, no matter how hard
the wind blows she is never
blown away."

Jaddah – Bedouin Grandmother   83

Jiddah-Bedouin Grandfather

84

This Bedouin man was standing at the foot of a Pyramid beside his camel that was loaded with two water jugs. From 7 am to 6 pm he earned his living by carrying water from a village near the Pyramids to a summering place for wealthy Cairenes. The cabins did not have electricity or running water because they were in the antiquities area. On the cabin roofs were water tanks that the vendor filled from his jugs. Gravity created water pressure that enabled the owners to have "running water."

Camels

Camels were only introduced to the Sahara desert circa 200 CE. They are a perfect fit for the desert: their soft feet and spreading toes keep them from sinking into the sand and they can go for more than two weeks without water.

Bedouins love their camels who provide so much to support their lives: milk, meat, skins for tents, transportation for trade goods and people, and plenty of entertainment.

The Mahari is a racing camel with long straight legs. To make sure the camel will develop those perfect legs, a newborn camel is held over a pit while sand is poured into it. The little legs dangle straight down into the pit, so that when the pit is full of sand, the baby is held secure by the sand and his little legs firm up straight.

After a few days he is dug out.

Tender Care in the Desert

This mother was very protective of her baby
and threatened us when we got too close.

85

Family Portrait   I couldn't resist this rare shot of camels' heads from many angles. This quartet was on the   86
back of a flatbed truck, which necessitated that they stand unusually close to each other.

Ready for the Show   This camel is elaborately shaved and   87
decorated for a village celebration.

A Visit to Borg El-Arab

Judge Jasper Brinton was the legal advisor at the American Embassy. He loved Borg el-Arab and wanted me to meet Bramley Bey, its creator.

One autumn day, my wife and I finally took him up on his offer to visit. We left his house in the Borg and crossed a courtyard where a flock of doves were gathered around Bramley Bey. The founder of the village was very proud of his doves and loved to come out to feed them.

This was a great photographic opportunity for me, but I had only one shot left in my camera. I asked my wife to clap her hands at my signal. At the unexpected sound, the doves, as one unit, rose up and flew over the walls.

This shot goes beyond the cliché that a flight of doves suggests peace. It symbolized the timelessness of the beautiful little village and the hope it offered the Egyptians of a desert that might someday bloom.

It was a magical day.

Borg el-Arab South Gate, Bab el-Malek

King Fouad Memorial Fountain   Built to honor the birth of his son, Prince Farouk.   89

Flight of Doves in Borg el-Arab Courtyard   90

Biographies of My Team

Frank Addington

Frank Addington's design and art direction work has been nationally recognized for its elegance and artistry. A native of the Kansas City area, Frank received his BFA in Design from the University of Kansas and began his career with Centron Films. After eight years as Art Director with West Associates Advertising and Design, he was appointed Senior Designer and Creative Director in the Kansas City office of Fleishman-Hillard, then the nation's largest independent public relations firm.

Frank has been a frequent guest lecturer in design at the University of Kansas since he started his own firm in 1992. He has worked with many notable clients including Hallmark Cards and the Nelson Atkins Museum of Art. His designs have been published in a number of annuals and magazines and have received awards from several local and national organizations including the Printing Institute of America.

Frank has been a vital member of Jack Jonathan's publishing team since 2001 when he designed Stowers Innovations, *Yes, You Can... Raise Financially Aware Kids*. He was the book designer of all six of the *Yes, You Can* series. We are delighted to have him join us once again to design *Egypt, The Eternal Spirit of Its People: Stories of an Exhibition*.

Steve Barr

Steve Barr, a Kansas City native, graduated from the University of Kansas with a Bachelor's Degree. Following graduation he began working in the lithographic industry. Throughout his career he has dealt with every aspect of creating and preparing artwork and text for prepress production. He is very skillful in scanning, photography, and the color enhancement and printing of digital images.

He began working with Jack Jonathan in 2001, digitizing a lifetime of photography from Jack's immense library of negatives. In 2004 he collaborated with Jack to produce the photographs for his exhibition *Light is the Eye of the Mind*. Since then, Steve has worked on most of the photographic projects that Jack has pursued as part of his philanthropic outreach. Some of these projects include the Children's Mercy Hospital installation, *Healing Images*, card projects, exhibitions, and donations of prints for auction.